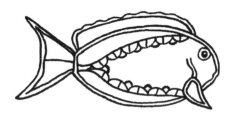

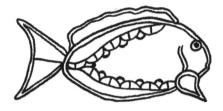

Georgie Woolridge

Waterlife

A Mindful Coloring Book

St. Martin's Griffin
New York

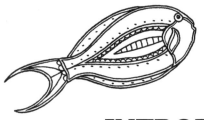

INTRODUCTION

The sea has always fascinated me. The wonderful feeling of serenity I get from just sitting and watching the waves gently lap against the shore is the exact same relaxation that I find in drawing.

While traveling in Asia I was lucky enough to swim underwater several times, but the one adventure that really sticks in my mind was a snorkeling trip in the Gili Islands near Bali. The boat took us pretty far out from the beach, so I was a bit nervous about the depth of the sea at first. The excitement of being there, however, soon took over and I was quickly over the edge of the boat. We started out as a group, but as time passed we drifted away in our own directions following the beautiful sea life. I ended up alone and having a bit of trouble with water getting into my snorkel. I was about to head back to the boat, but for some reason I decided to give it one last go. I put my head back under the water and I couldn't believe what I was seeing—there was a beautiful turtle swimming right toward me! I swam with it for a while until

it disappeared into the depths of the coral reef. I managed to capture it on my underwater camera not realizing beforehand that I only had two pictures left! It was a truly amazing memory that will last a lifetime. As you can imagine, that turtle had to feature in my book.

As well as the feeling I get when I am near the sea, the rainbow of colors and dreamy sense of movement beneath the surface really capture my imagination. The wild abundance of different creatures with so many unusual shapes and patterns continuously inspires me. Whether I am sketching the ethereal motion of the Pacific sea nettle, penciling in the gruff face of the giant grouper, or drawing a sweetly comic

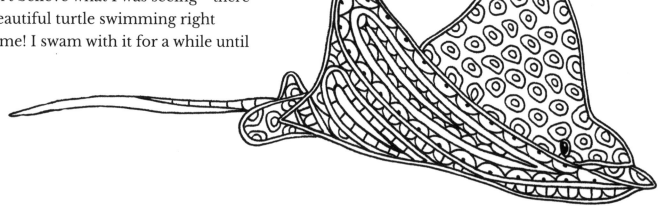

spotted trunkfish, I am in my element. From the brilliant azure seas where bottlenose dolphins caper, to the inky blue depths where seahorses gracefully twirl, I hope I have managed to capture a snapshot of the world's most extraordinary underwater creatures in this collection.

A few of the designs in this book are very intricate and might require a fine pencil or pen, or you could choose simply to color over these parts of the patterns leaving the black lines to show through your coloring—either option will certainly look very beautiful. When coloring my own designs, I use a variety of ProMarker pens and watercolor, but I also love to blend different mediums together to create beautiful effects. Sometimes the vividness of pen over the subtle colors of crayons, pencils, chalks, and pastels really adds to the final outcome—but you can use any method you choose.

There is nothing more soothing or satisfying than watching an underwater animal in its natural environment, and I really hope you enjoy this underwater universe as much as I do. So sit back, relax, and spend some time in the dreamy world of *Waterlife*.

Georgie Woolridge

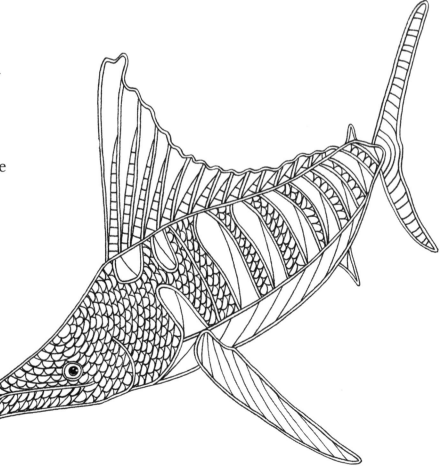

SEAHORSE

('siːhɔːs,' *Hippocampus*)

Seahorses are found in tropical and temperate waters around the world. There
are more than fifty-four known species, ranging in size from ½ in to 14 in
(1.5 cm to 35.5 cm). Seahorses are the only animal species where the male carries
the unborn young, gestating the eggs in their brood pouch. Seahorses move around
by using a tiny fin on their back that flutters up to thirty-five times per second.

GREEN SEA TURTLE

('griːn si tərdl,' *Chelonia mydas*)

Green sea turtles are so named because of the color of their fat and cartilage rather than their shells, which are usually brown or olive, and occasionally black. They can grow to more than 3 ft (1 m) in length and inhabit tropical and subtropical waters all over the world. They travel immense distances between their feeding grounds and their hatching beaches, with some turtles swimming more than 1,600 miles (2,600 km).

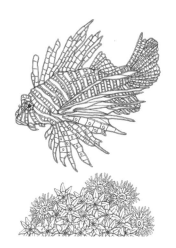

LIONFISH
('lʌɪənfɪ∫,' *Pterois volitans*)

With its unusually long and resplendent fins, the lionfish creates a display around its head and body of dark orange and white stripes, resembling a mane. The equally beautiful fins on its back, however, can deliver a shot of powerful venom, although these are generally used only in self-defense. The lionfish uses its ornate appearance to disguise itself among the coral, waiting to pounce on passing fish and shrimp. Lionfish can grow up to 15 in (40 cm) in length.

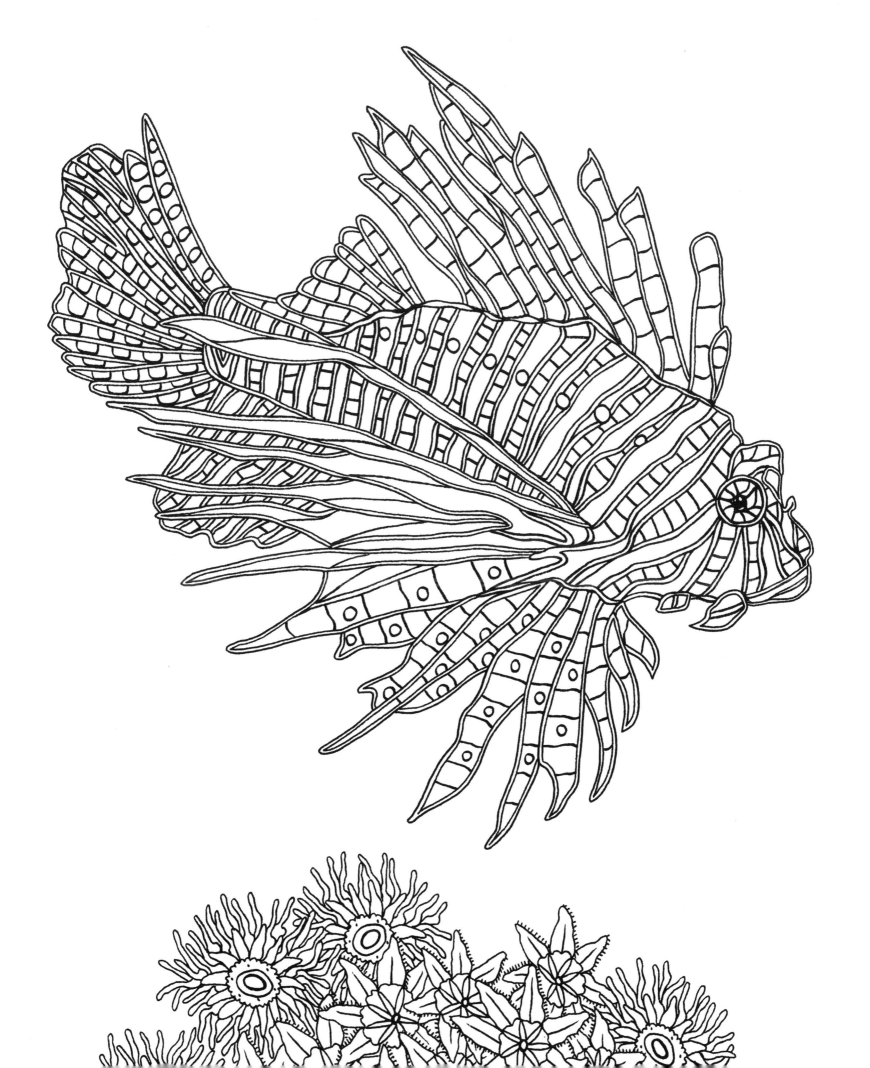

BOTTLENOSE DOLPHIN
(ˈbɒt(ə)lnəʊz dɒlfɪn,' *Tursiops truncatus*)

Naturally sociable by nature, bottlenose dolphins swim in packs called "pods," communicating with each other in a language of whistles, squeaks, and body movements, working as a team to catch their fish. The color of their skin is a camouflage: when viewed from above, the upper body blends with the blue-gray depths of the ocean, while their white bellies, if viewed from below, mimic the white glare of the surface. Bottlenose dolphins can grow as large as 14 ft (4 m) long, and their upturned mouths give the impression of a perpetual smile.

COCONUT OCTOPUS

('kəʊkənʌt ɒktəpəs,' *Amphioctopus marginatus*)

The coconut octopus measures just 6 in (15 cm) in diameter (including its eight legs) and is found in shallow, tropical waters, moving slowly along the sandy bottom, feeding on crabs and shrimp. It is usually a dark orange color with a frill of white suckers that resemble coral. Its soft, velvety body means it's defenseless to attack, so to protect itself it rolls into a ball, winding six legs around its head, and using the remaining two to keep moving. This octopus also cleverly picks up discarded coconut shells to use as protection.

PEACOCK MANTIS SHRIMP
('piːkɒk mantɪs ʃrɪmp,' *Odontodactylus scyllarus*)

The peacock mantis shrimp lives among the colorful Pacific coral reefs, and is famous for its radiant, multicolored shell, mottled with neon-bright shades of red, blue, orange, and green. It can grow up to 7 in (18 cm) long, but it can still attack prey bigger than itself, delivering an incredibly fast blow with its arms shooting out faster than the blink of an eye. It has eyes on stalks that not only move independently of each other, but also can detect many more colors than the human eye, including ultraviolet light.

ORIENTAL SWEETLIPS
('ɔːrɪ'ɛnt(ə) swiːtlɪps,' *Plectorhinchus vittatus*)

Oriental sweetlips are found in the coral reefs of the Indian Ocean. They're part of a species known as "grunts"; fish that make a sound by grinding their teeth plates together and that have oversize rubberlike lips. They're characterized by their unusual spots and stripes: their bodies are adorned with thin black-and-white stripes while their fins are spotted with black polka dots on yellow. Their pattern changes as they age, and young fish are marked with thin stripes on their tails, which then transform into black dots as an adult.

CORAL TROUT
('kɒr(ə)l traʊt,' *Plectropomus leopardus*)

The coral trout is found around the coral reefs of the western Pacific Ocean. Its beautiful orange color is mottled with blue leopardlike spots, mimicking the reef it swims in. When opened, its mouth is huge with rows of razor-sharp teeth. The fish feed on shrimp and other reef fish, and have been known to grow up to 3 ft (1 m) in length. All coral trout are born female, but they change sex to male as they age, usually after spawning.

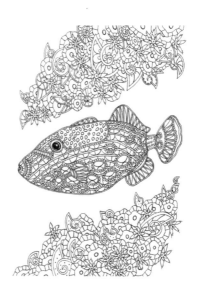

CLOWN TRIGGERFISH
(ˈklaʊn trɪɡəfɪ ʃ,ˈ *Balistoides conspicillum*)

The remarkable neon-bright coloring of the clown triggerfish make it one of the species most threatened by the aquarium trade. The lower part of its oval body is patterned with large, white spots and its mouth is outlined in bright yellow. An intricate, almost leopardlike yellow pattern tessellates across its upper body. Usually found in tropical waters around steep reef drops, the clown triggerfish can appear to glide without moving because it uses its small upper and lower fins rather than its tail to swim.

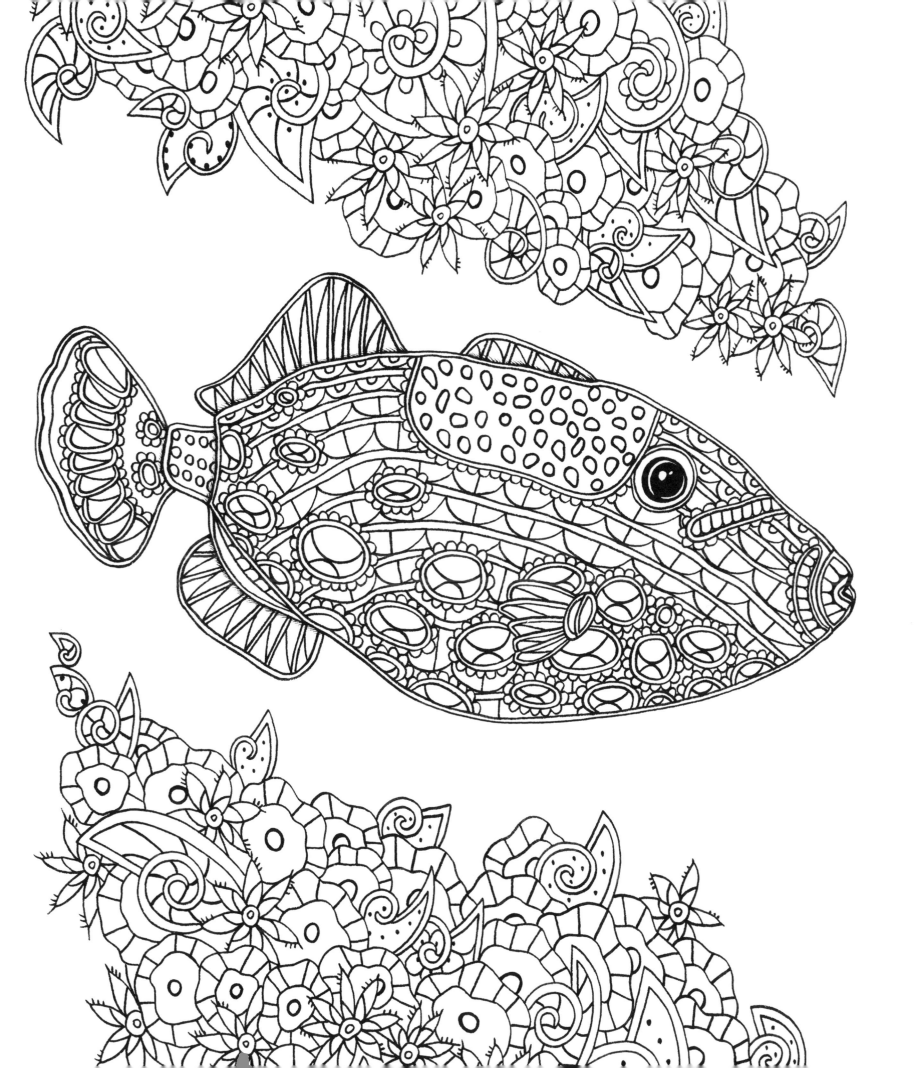

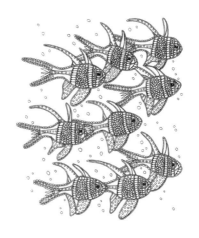

BANGGAI CARDINALFISH

('baŋ-gʌɪ kɑːd(ɪ)n(ə)lfɪʃ,' *Pterapogon kauderni*)

These small and ornate fish are named after their main habitat, the Banggai Islands of Indonesia, where they exist in dwindling numbers, being highly sought after for home aquariums. Small but perfectly formed, they grow to only 3 in (8 cm) in length. Their pale yellow bodies are adorned with black vertical stripes with a white lining and their fins fork out in a pleasing array, with minute white dots at the tips. When the female cardinalfish has produced her eggs, the male stores them in his mouth for an incubation period of thirty days.

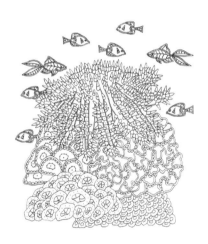

CROWN OF THORNS STARFISH
('kraʊn ɒf θɔːn stɑːfɪʃ,' *Acanthaster planci*)

This prickly starfish is known for its coat of spiky thorns, and each spike is covered with venom. Unlike a typical five-armed starfish, the crown of thorns can have up to twenty-one arms, making it more disk-shaped in appearance. It can grow up to 30 in (80 cm) in diameter. Its underside is soft and moves fluidly across the coral, which is its main source of food. It smothers the coral, which it digests directly on contact with its stomach, leaving just a skeleton behind. In color it can vary from a light gray-green to a more lurid purple or pink.

SPOTTED EAGLE RAY
('spɒtɪd iːg(ə)l reɪ,' *Aetobatus narinari*)

The spotted eagle ray is distinguishable by its two huge "wings" (fins) with which it moves gracefully through the water. It has a long black whiplike tail making its total length as long as 10 ft (3 m). There are several poisonous spines along the base of its tail, which can be lethal. The top half of its flat body is deep blue or black, speckled with white dots, while its underbelly is white. The eagle ray is sometimes known to launch itself out of the water in a characteristic jump.

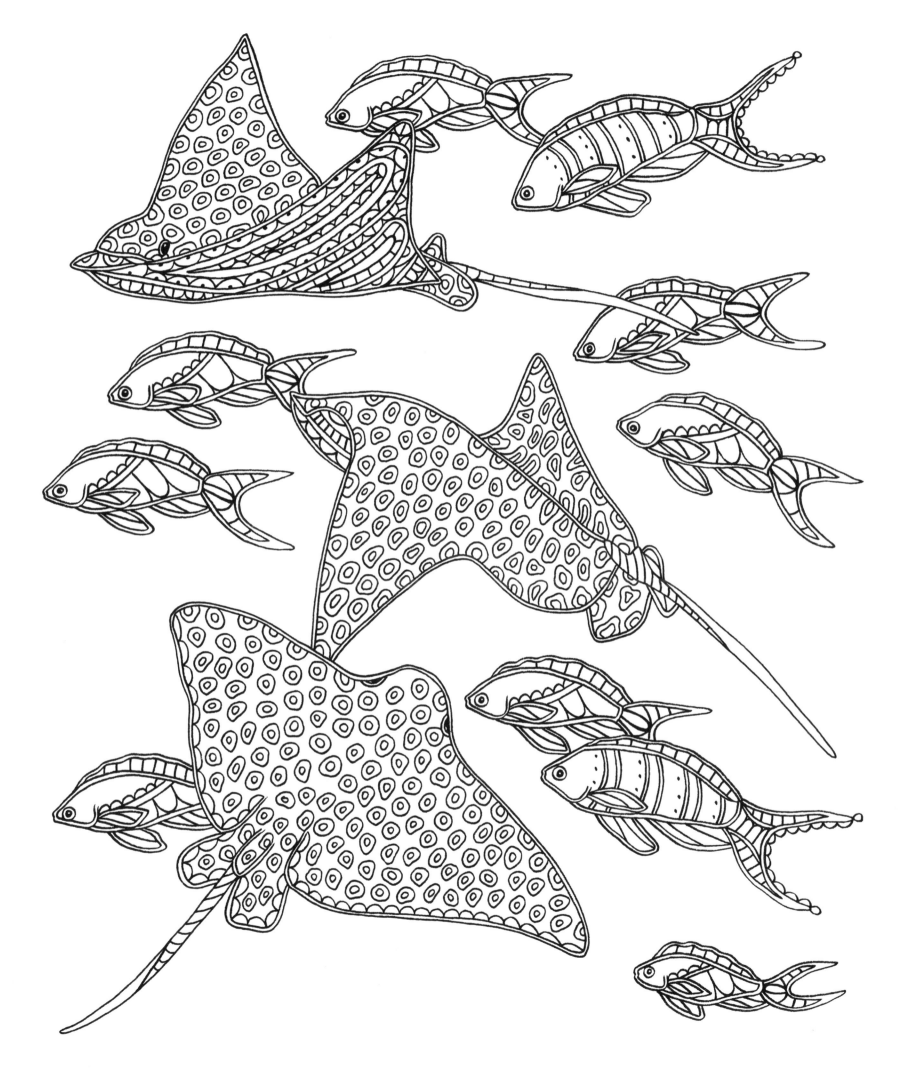

SPOTTED TRUNKFISH
('spɒtɪd trʌŋkfɪʃ,' *Lactophrys bicaudalis*)

The spotted trunkfish is characterized by its strange box-shaped body and pronounced hooded eyes. Its beautiful golden-yellow scales are covered with black dots. It can grow up to 18 in (48 cm) in size. To ward off predators, this fish has two sharp spines by its tail fin and, when touched, it releases a poison from its skin that is only lethal when ingested. If eaten, it's able to kill a predator as large as a shark.

BLUE DISCUS FISH
('bluː discus fɪʃ,' *Symphysodon aequifasciatus*)

Named on account of its circular, disk-shaped body that shimmers with iridescent stripes of brilliant colors such as cobalt blue, fiery red, turquoise, and orange, the discus fish is in demand by the aquarium trade. Usually found in the Amazon River basin, this fish lives in shoals among submerged tree roots and branches in which it makes its home. When it hatches eggs, it also creates a secretion from its skin, which its larvae live on, so it's not uncommon to see an adult discus fish with many tiny fish attached to its body.

ORANGE CLOWNFISH
('ɒrɪn(d)ʒ klaʊnfɪʃ,' *Amphiprion percula*)

Aside from its striking orange-and-white striped body, the clownfish is also famous for its important reciprocal relationship with the anemone. Before making its home among them, it accustoms itself by lightly stroking different parts of its skin on their tentacles. While the anemone offers the clownfish morsels of food and shelter from prey, the clownfish in return repels invaders and grooms the anemone to rid it of parasites. All clownfish are born male, but are able to change sex to female if the only breeding female dies.

DUGONG

(ˈduːɡɒŋ,' *Dugong dugon*)

The dugong (which comes from the Malay, meaning "lady of the sea") is of closer relation to the elephant than any marine mammal. It can grow up to 10 ft long (3 m) and weighs around 926 lb (420 kg). As an herbivore, its habitat is limited to coastal areas with seagrass meadows where it sucks up vegetation with its square-shaped mouth. The dugong is usually a pale white color as a baby, but changes to soft gray, then a deeper gray-blue to brown as an adult.

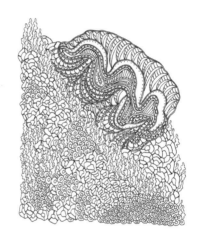

GIANT CLAM

('dʒʌɪənt klam,' *Tridacna gigas*)

The giant clam is the largest of the living mollusks: it can weigh more than 440 lb (200 kg) and grow to about 4 ft (1.2 m) wide. The clam can't close its shell, and often displays a glorious multicolor mantle; bright blues, greens, purples with a pale pink, white, or gray shell. It makes its home in coral reef, and once embedded there, it enjoys a symbiotic relationship with the algae that dwell among its tissue. While the clam allows the algae shelter and sunlight, the algae make protein and sugar for the clam to ingest and continue growing.

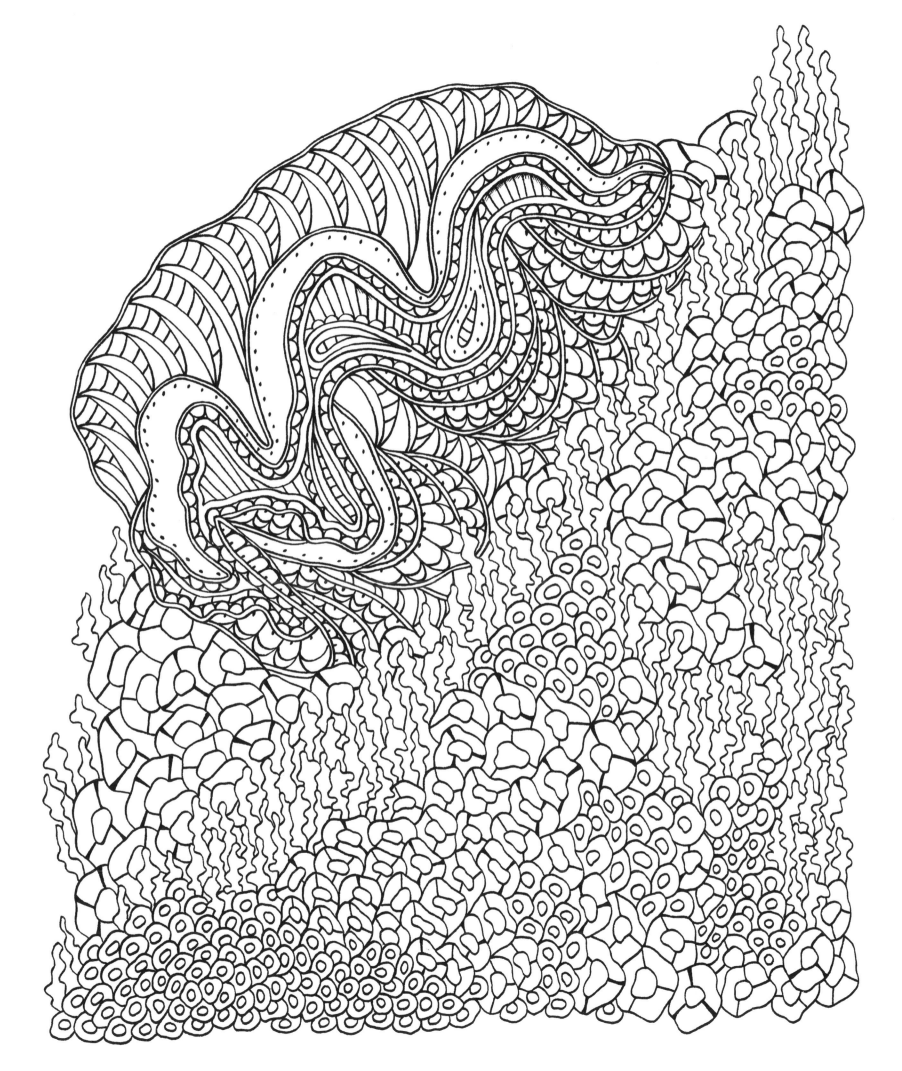

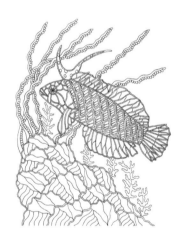

DRAGON WRASSE

('drag(ə)n ras,' *Novaculichthys taeniourus*)

The dragon wrasse is also known as the "rockmover" because of its ability to
turn over small stones in search of food. It can grow up to 12 in (30 cm) in length.
Unusually, the juvenile and adult fish are almost completely different in appearance.
The juvenile looks a little urchin-like, with its black and white intricately patterned
body, outlined by ragged feathery fins and two long antennae-like fins above its
eyes. Adults lose these fins and have a much neater body of dark green scales with
white dots. They have a white stripe on their tail fin and black lines around the eye,
resembling long eyelashes.

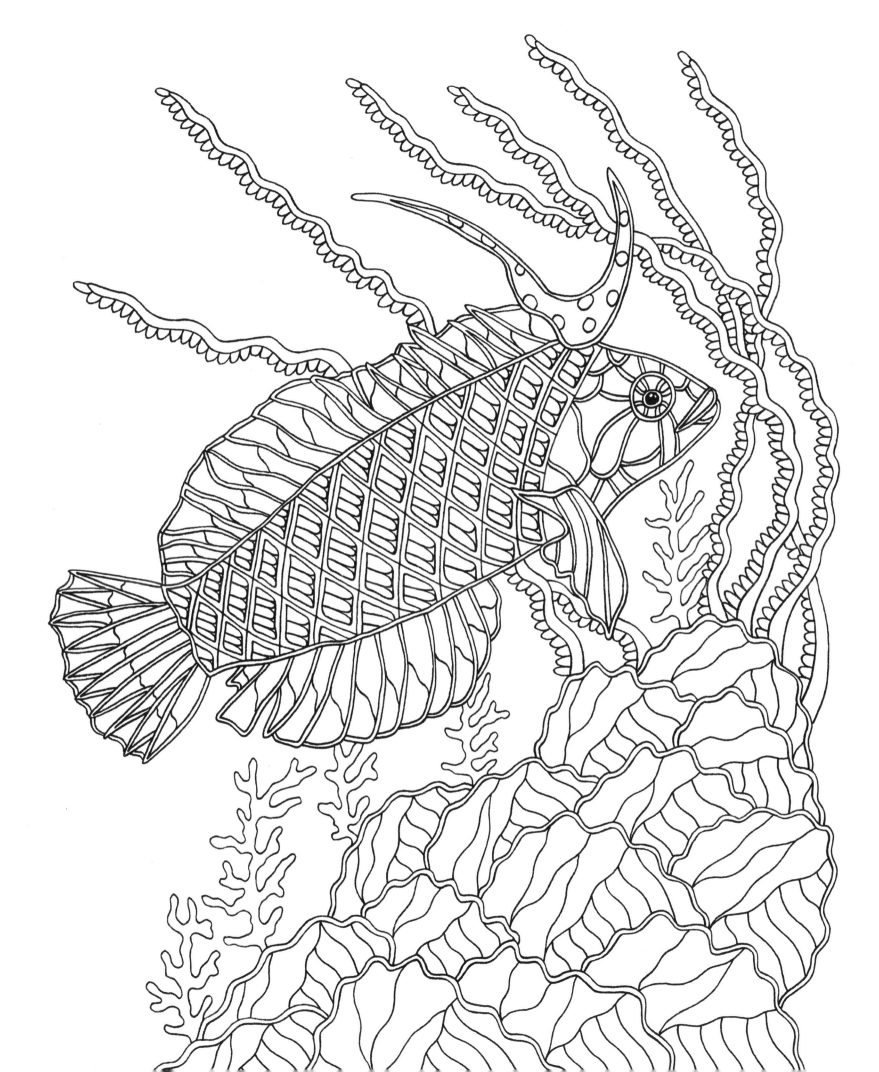

EMPEROR ANGELFISH
('ɛmp(ə)rə angelfɪʃ,' *Pomacanthus imperator*)

Found in the Indian and Pacific Oceans, the emperor angelfish lives among coral reefs and exhibits a dazzling array of color: electric blue and bright yellow horizontal stripes with dark purple fins and a blue-black "mask" that covers its eyes. Their extreme appearance makes them particularly visible to predators, but their habitat among exotic coral offers some protection. Emperor angelfish feed on algae, sponges, and small invertebrates, and their strong jaws are even able to break up hard coral. When they mate, they swim quickly up to the surface in order to disperse their eggs on the current.

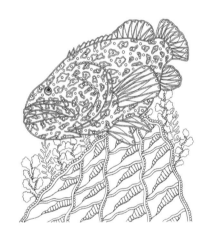

GIANT GROUPER
('dʒʌɪənt gruːpə,' *Epinephelus lanceolatus*)

The giant grouper is also known as a "bumblebee" grouper, due to its distinctive yellow-and-black color palette and the mottled yellow dots that cover its scales. As the fish ages, the yellow patches become more ornate. It has a large jutting mouth and a pretty yellow spotted tail fin. It lives in coral reefs and can grow up to 8.2 ft (2.5 m). In Chinese culture, this fish is generally associated with good luck and is thought to have medicinal properties.

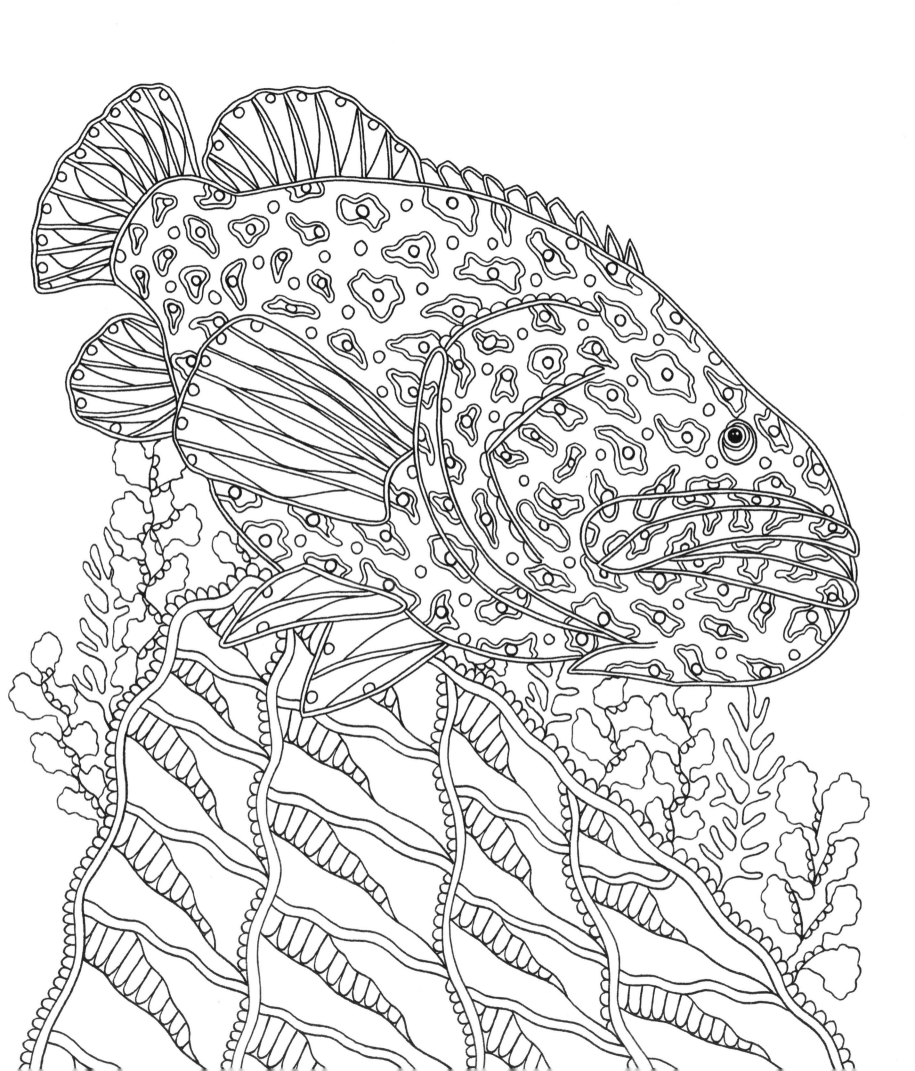

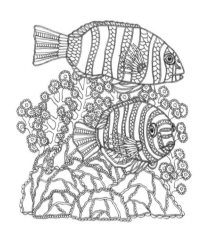

HARLEQUIN TUSKFISH
('hɑːlɪkwɪn tʌskfɪ∫,' *Choerodon fasciatus*)

The harlequin tuskfish is found in the coral reefs of the western Pacific Ocean. As its name suggests, it is known for its brilliant multicolored coat of blue, green, and orange. Other distinguishing features are its protruding blue teeth with which it can rip through invertebrates such as crustaceans. The harlequin tuskfish can grow as large as 12 in (30 cm). Younger tuskfish have "false eye spots" (known as *ocelli*) around their fins. The *ocelli* are photosensitive and allow the fish to notice changes of light in their vicinity, which could signal a predator.

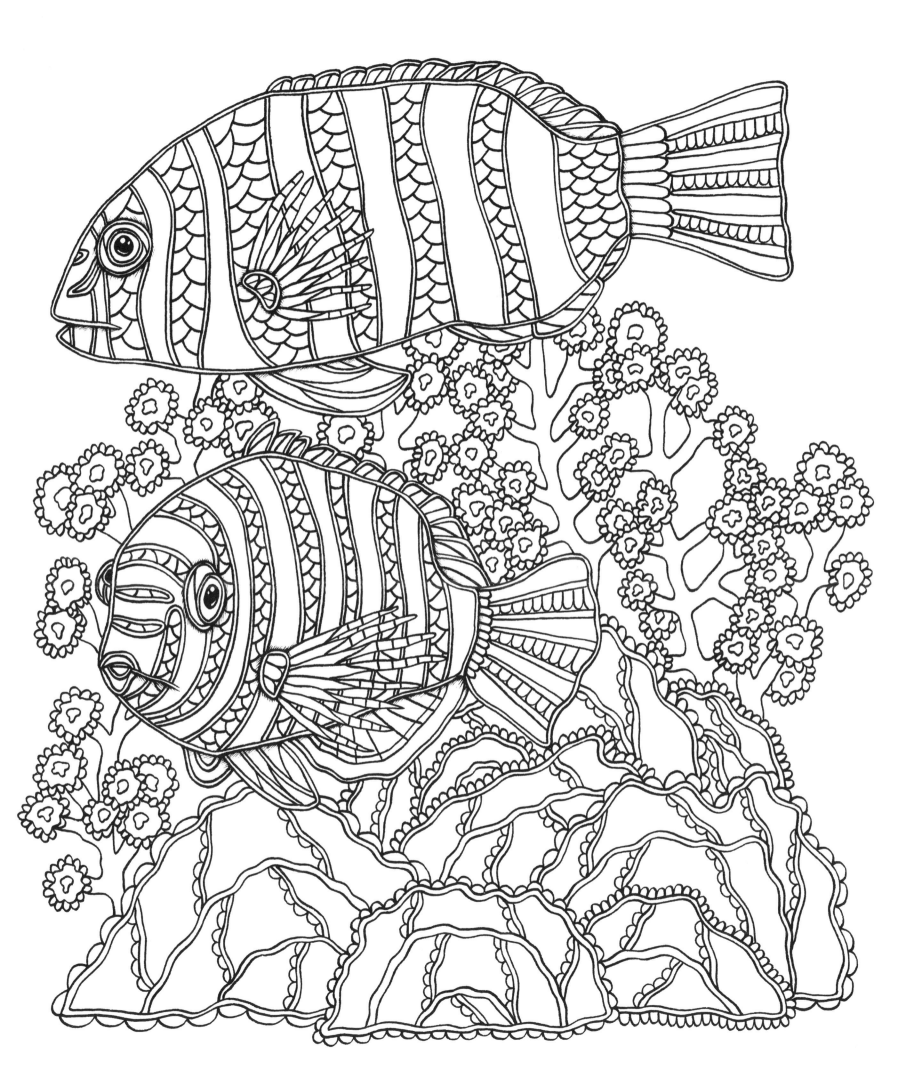

HERMIT CRAB
('hɜːmɪt krab,' *Dardanus calidus*)

The hermit crab is lobsterlike in appearance, with a brightly colored orange shell. Its body, or more precisely, its stomach, however, is curved around in a spiral shape and does not have a shell, which means it is exposed to predators. To remedy this, the hermit crab finds an abandoned seashell, or anything else on the seabed with a similar shape, and uses it as a "mobile home." Its stomach has an especially strong grip on the end, which clasps the found shell to keep it in place. As the crab grows, it must find bigger shells. The hermit crab is predominantly nocturnal and some species can live for up to seventy years.

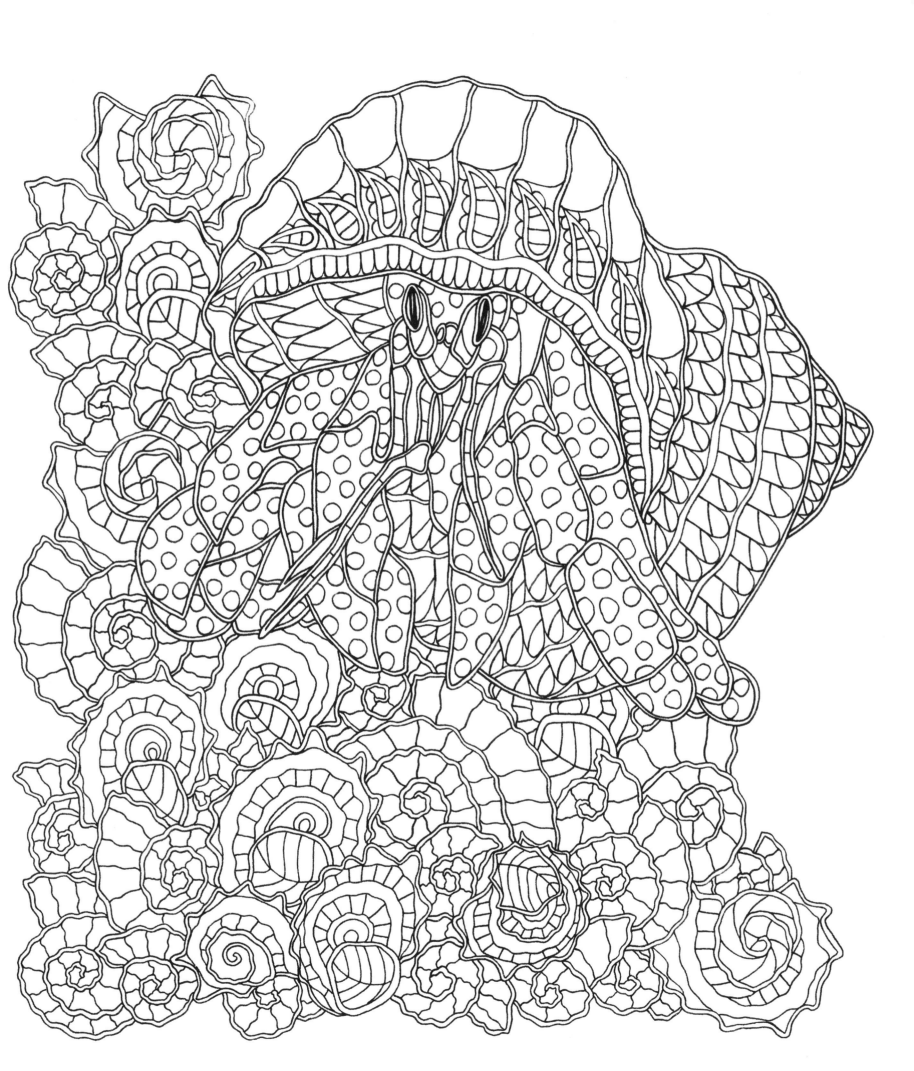

LEAFY SEADRAGON

('liːfi siːdrag(ə)n,' *Phycodurus eques*)

The leafy seadragon is part of the same family as the seahorse and its incredible "leafy" shape makes it almost indistinguishable from seaweed or plants such as kelp. It can grow up to 14 in (35 cm) in total, its body consisting of leaflike branches in brown, yellow, and orange. Although it appears to float through the water like a plant, it actually has small fins on the upper and rear body. Leafy seadragons are now approaching endangered species status because their habitat is threatened by pollution.

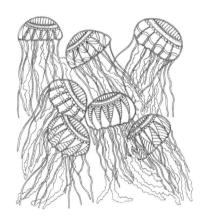

PACIFIC SEA NETTLE
(ˈpəˈsɪfɪk siː nɛt(ə)l,ˈ *Chrysaora fuscescens*)

One of the most stunning jellyfish species, the Pacific sea nettle has a gorgeous yet delicate yellow body with deep red stringlike outer tentacles and beautiful streams of ruffled white inner tentacles that resemble trails of blossom. It uses its tentacles like a net, amassing food as it passes by while delivering a potent sting, which is poisonous but not lethal. These tentacles can grow up to 16 ft (4.8 m) long and they start the digesting process as they pass the food up to the mouth.

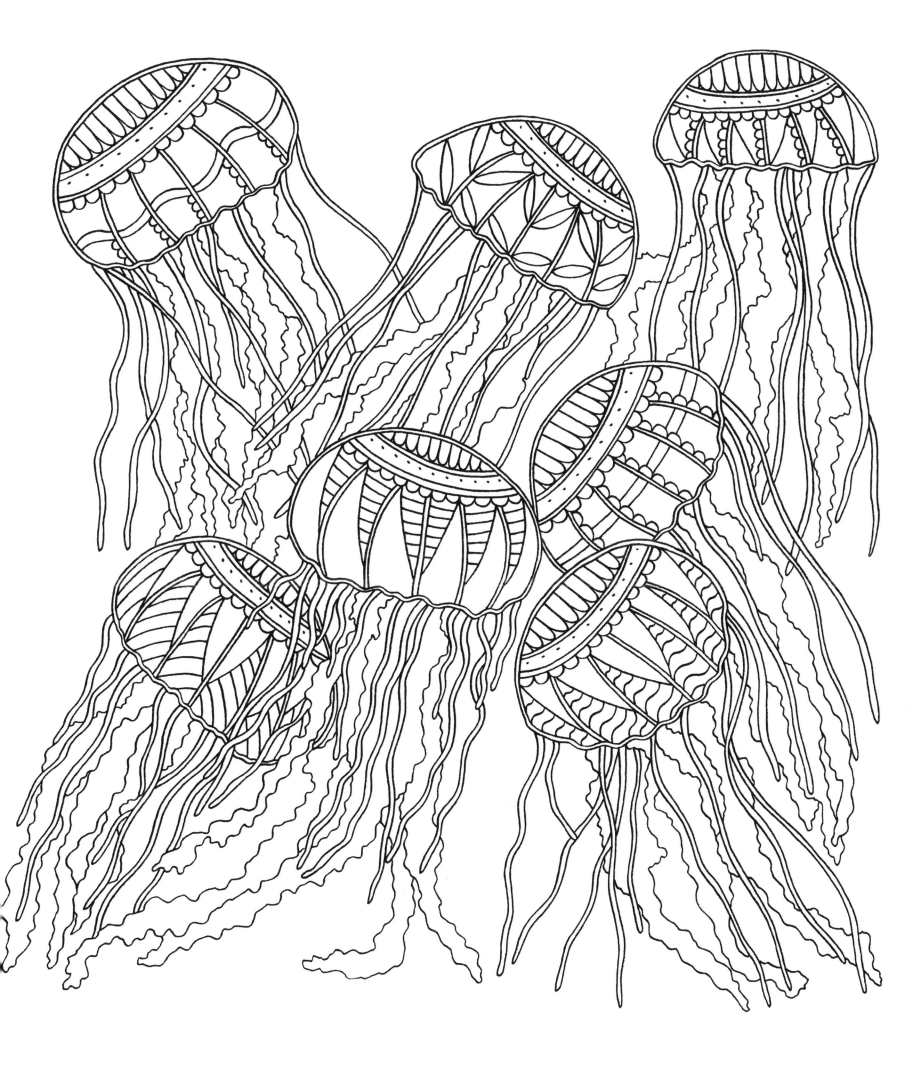

BIGFIN REEF SQUID

('bɪgfɪn riːf skwɪd,' *Sepioteuthis lessoniana*)

The bigfin reef squid has oversize eyes, arms with rows of suckers, and a large oval fin that extends around its body. It can vary in color from translucent white to yellow, pink, or violet. Its skin contains light-reflecting cells so that it can quickly change body color and pattern to be able to camouflage itself. It is remarkable for its incredibly quick growth rate, growing to 1.3 lb (600 g) in only four months. However, it also has a very short lifespan of only 315 days. The bigfin reef squid swims in schools and is attracted by light.

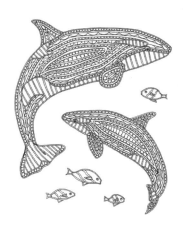

KILLER WHALE
('kɪlə weɪl,' *Orcinus orca*)

Able to survive in all climates, the killer whale is found in both the cold Arctic Ocean as well as tropical seas. It can grow up to 30 ft (9 m) long and is known for its rows of incredibly sharp teeth and clever methods of hunting. It eats fish, sharks, turtles, and birds, either herding its prey to the surface and giving it powerful blows with a tail fin, or holding it down so that it suffocates. Killer whales often breach the surface of the ocean, performing jumps and tail slaps to interact, woo, or just play with each other.

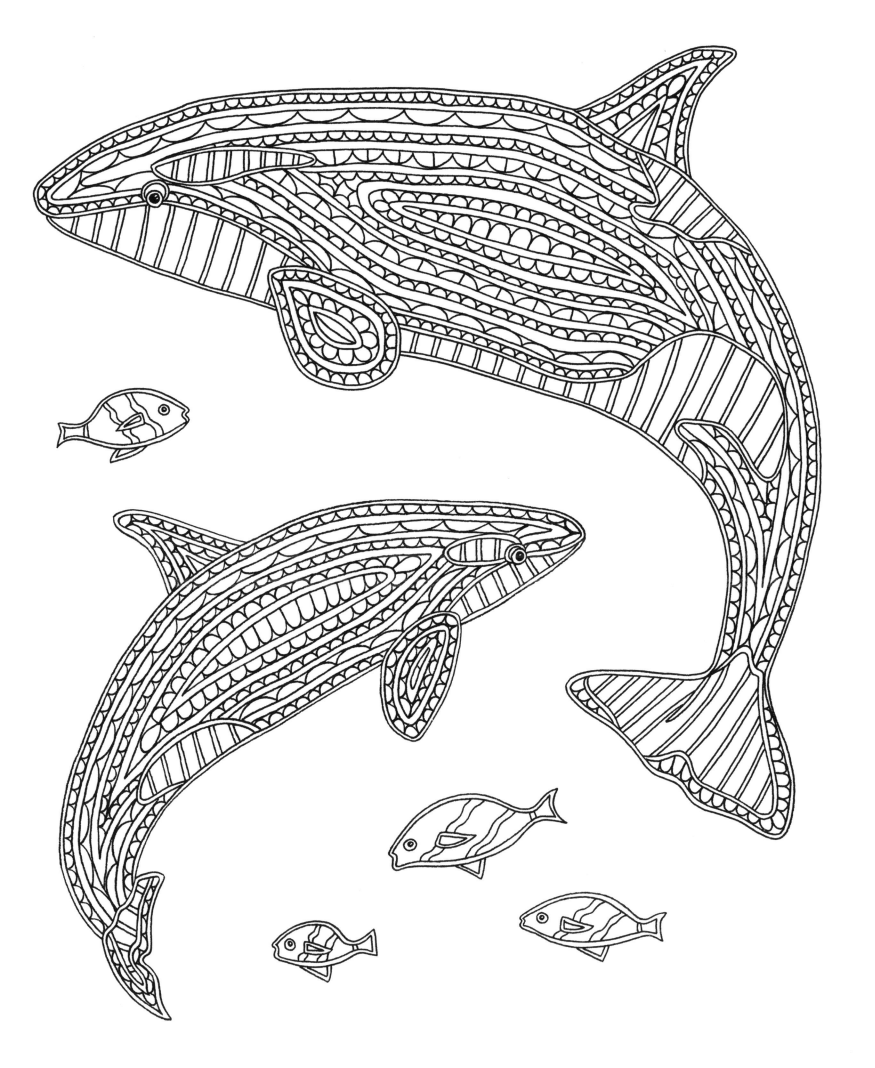

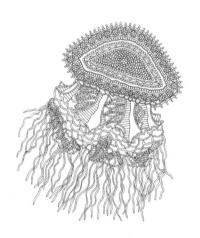

LION'S MANE JELLYFISH
(ˈlʌɪən meɪn dʒɛlɪfɪʃ,ˈ *Cyanea capillata*)

This large species of jellyfish is known for its long, flowing red and yellow manelike tentacles, of which there are more than 800, some even reaching lengths of 120 ft (37 m). The lion's mane jellyfish can vary in color from red or purple to orange. It survives on a diet of plankton, other jellyfish, small fish, and shrimp, which it immobilizes with a sting from its tentacles. It uses pulsations to move slowly through the water and relies on currents to move greater distances.

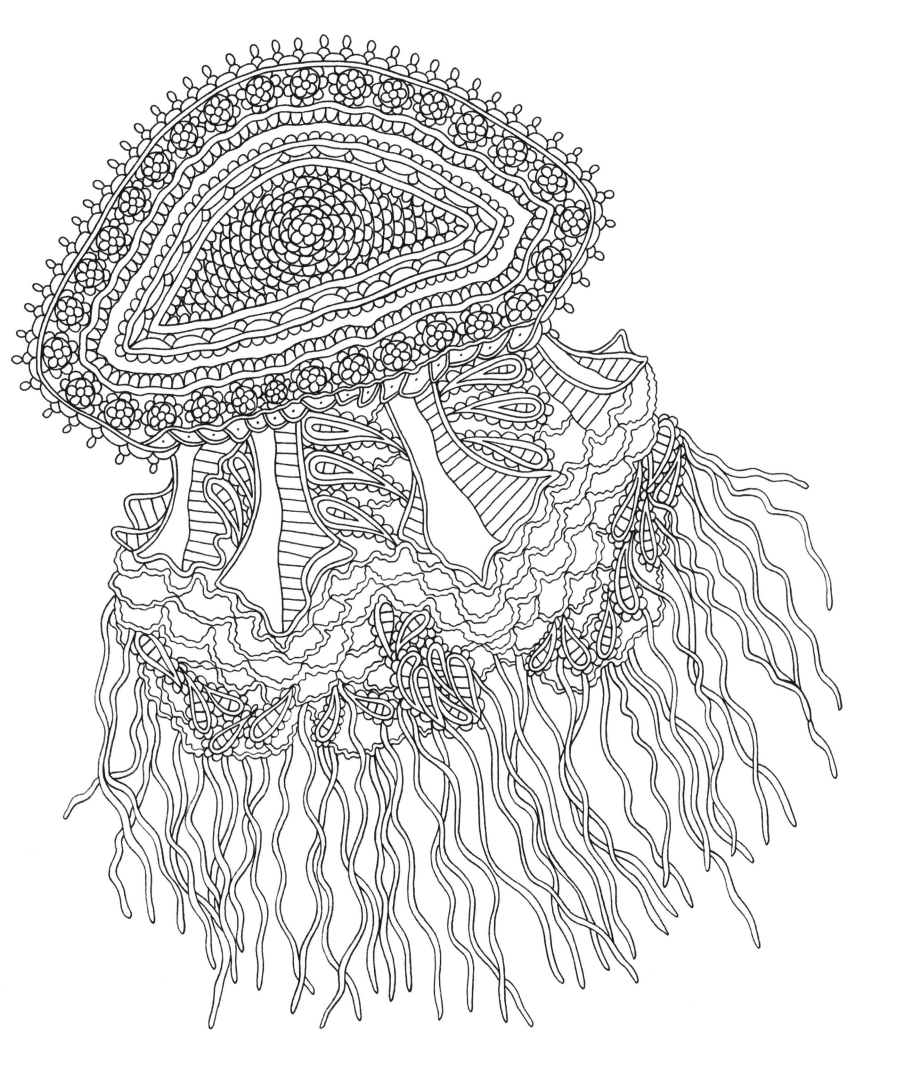

ATLANTIC MACKEREL
(ˈatˈlantɪk mak(ə)r(ə)l,ˈ *Scomber scombrus*)

Atlantic mackerel typically swim in dense schools of many thousands, creating
a beautiful visual effect when seen through the water. The upper body is a darkish
green or blue with wavy stripes, and the lower body shimmers with a silvery,
brassy iridescence. The mackerel needs a lot of oxygen, so it swims continuously
with a swift sideways movement to channel enough water through its gills.
Mackerel breed close to the surface because their eggs float, but this also makes
them vulnerable to predators.

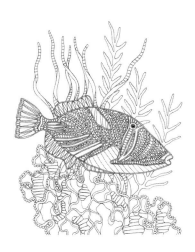

PICASSO TRIGGERFISH
(ˈpɪˈkasəʊ trɪɡəfɪʃ,' *Rhinecanthus aculeatus*)

The Picasso triggerfish has remarkably striking features, with eyes set far back on the body giving the impression of a huge mouth that is highlighted with a yellow stripe and a small blue "mustache." The body has further yellow, blue, and black striped markings and can grow up to 11 in (28 cm) in length. It is a territorial fish that fiercely guards its young and is known to maintain the same territory (sandy and coral reefs) for up to eight years.

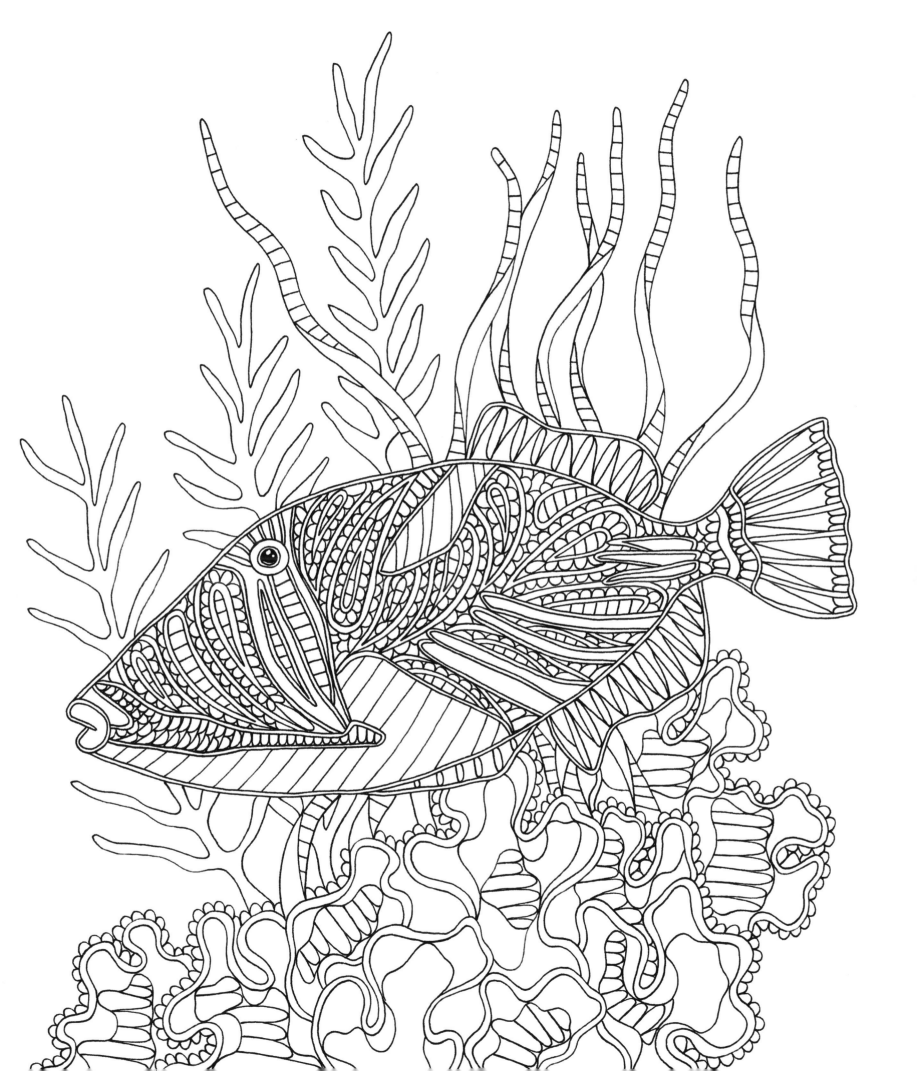

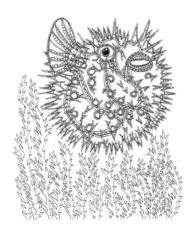

PUFFERFISH
(ˈpʌfəfɪʃ,' *Tetraodontidae*)

The pufferfish, as its name suggests, is known for its ability to inflate itself by quickly ingesting huge amounts of water when under threat. It can't get away from predators quickly, but it is poisonous when eaten, containing a toxin that is foul-tasting to fish and deadly to humans. Some species additionally have sharp spikes that protrude from their skin. They grow up to 2 ft (61 cm) in length and their teeth are molded together to form a hard gum to crush invertebrates.

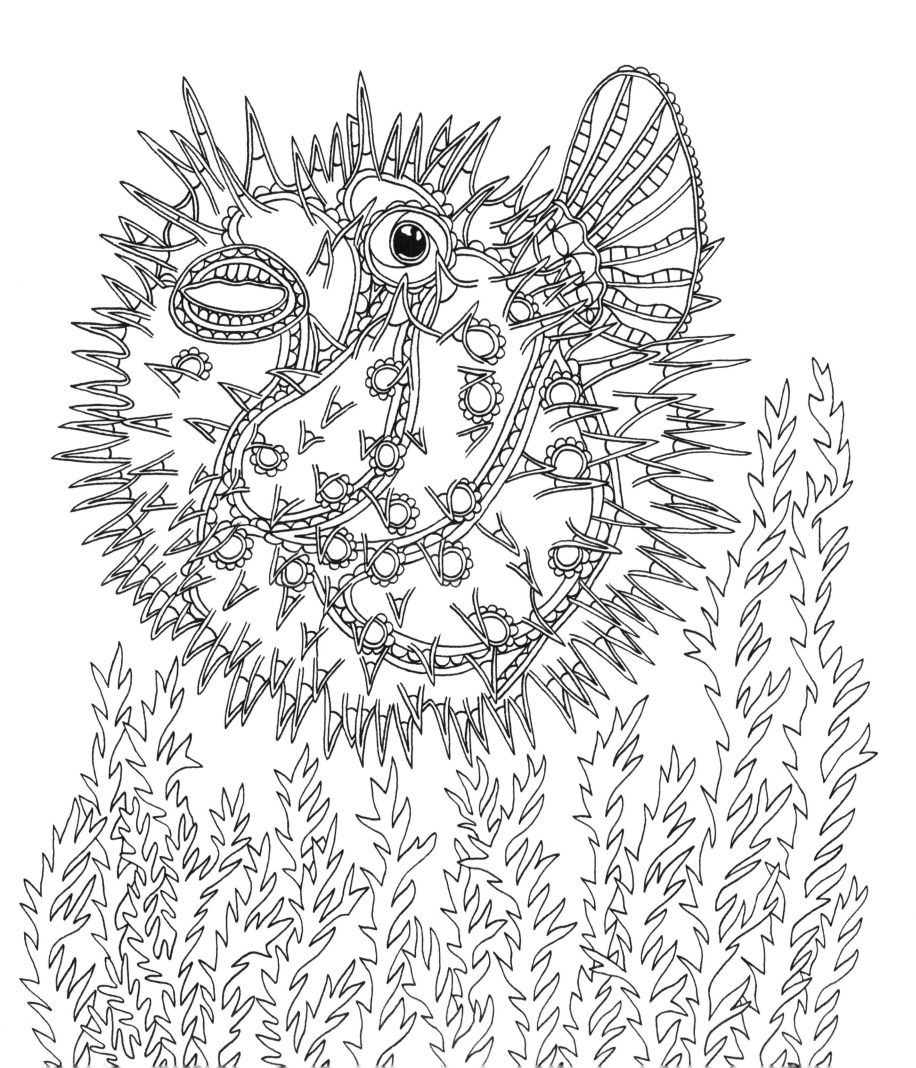

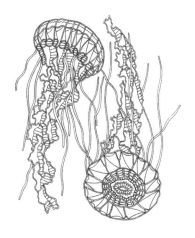

PURPLE STRIPED JELLYFISH
('pəːp(ə)l strʌɪpt dʒɛlɪfɪʃ,' *Chrysaora colorata*)

This beautiful jellyfish is known to exist solely in the Monterey Bay area off the California coast. It has ghostly white tentacles and remarkable deep purple radial stripes against a pale white body. It has frilly inner tentacles and stringlike outer tentacles. It can grow to 3 ft (1 m) in diameter and emits a painful sting from its tentacles if it comes into contact with prey or humans, but the sting is not lethal.

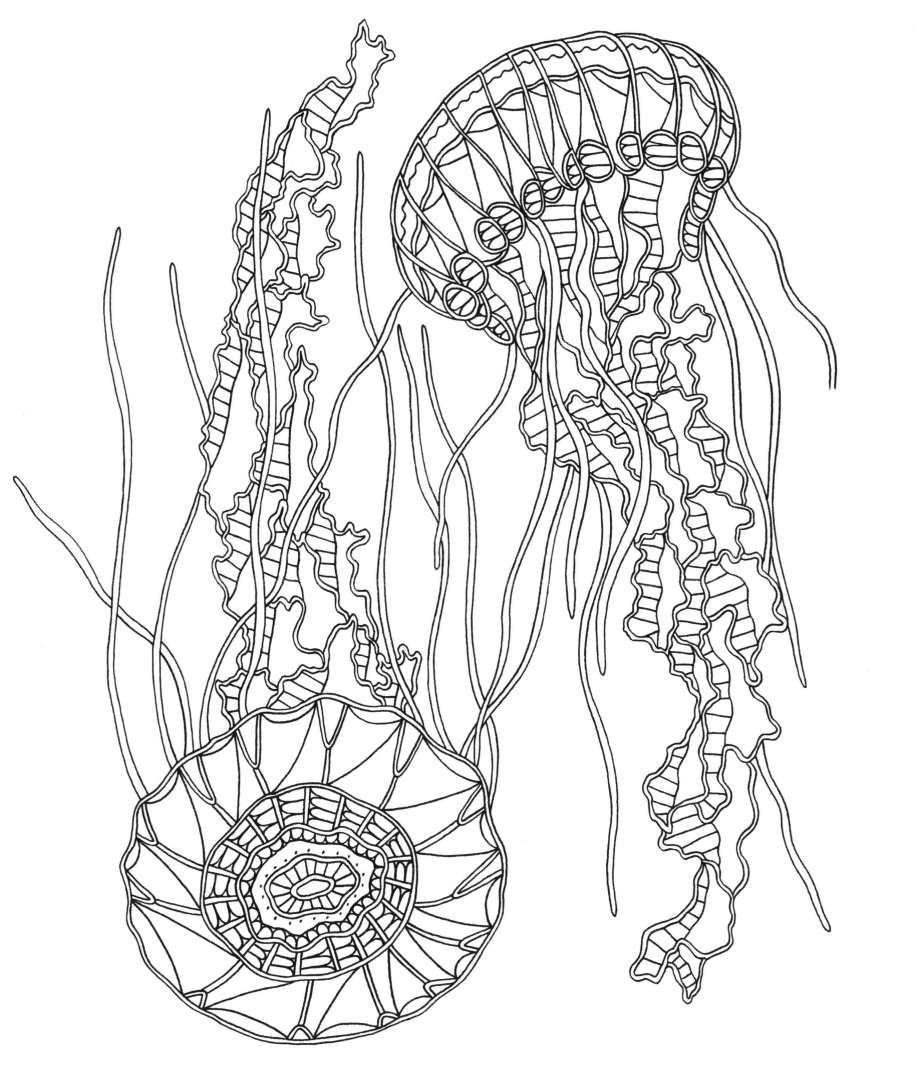

RACCOON BUTTERFLYFISH
('rəkuːn bʌtəflʌɪfɪʃ,' *Chaetodon lunula*)

Like its namesake, the eyes of the raccoon butterflyfish are surrounded by a black-and-white band that resembles a mask. Found in shallow tropical waters, it looks for shelter close to reef beds. It has a beautiful coloration of yellow, red, and gold stripes across its body and dark orange edging in an oval shape around the fins. Some also have a "false eyespot" that confuses predators who are fooled into attacking the tail rather than its face. It lives in cavelike areas and feeds on coral and anemone, growing to 8 in (20 cm) long.

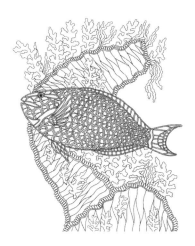

RAINBOW PARROTFISH
('reɪnbəʊ parətfɪʃ,' *Scarus guacamaia*)

Despite its bold color combinations and markings, the rainbow parrotfish is hard to classify because it changes color and pattern even within species; it can be green with yellow spots or even red with green spots. It grows to 3.9 ft (1.2 m) in length, and can also change sex numerous times within its lifetime. Most remarkably, in the dark some species cover themselves in a mucous produced from a gland on their head that makes them undetectable to nocturnal predators.

RIBBON EEL

(‘rɪb(ə)n iːl,’ *Rhinomuraena quaesita*)

Found in the Indo-Pacific Ocean, dwelling under sand, mud, or rocks, the ribbon eel changes color with age, beginning its life a dark color and eventually developing an electric blue body with bright yellow edging, giving it a ribbonlike appearance. It has very small teeth, a curious frill of skin on its nostrils, and tentacles on its lower jaw. The male ribbon eel can grow as long as 37 in (94 cm) in length. It is thought that all ribbon eels begin life as male, and then change sex to female as they mature.

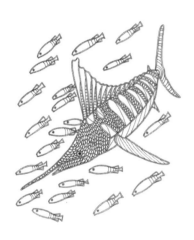

STRIPED MARLIN
('strʌɪpt mɑːlɪn,' *Kajikia audax*)

Known for its long, swordlike beak, the striped marlin is under threat from the fishing industry as it is commercially fished for sushi. It can grow to a maximum length of 14 ft (4.2 m) and reach a weight of 420 lb (190 kg), so is therefore also sought after by sports fishermen. The striped marlin is usually a beautiful blue-gray color, but when courting or feeding, its stripes become electric blue or phosphorescent. Preferring warmer waters, it migrates toward the equator in the cold seasons.

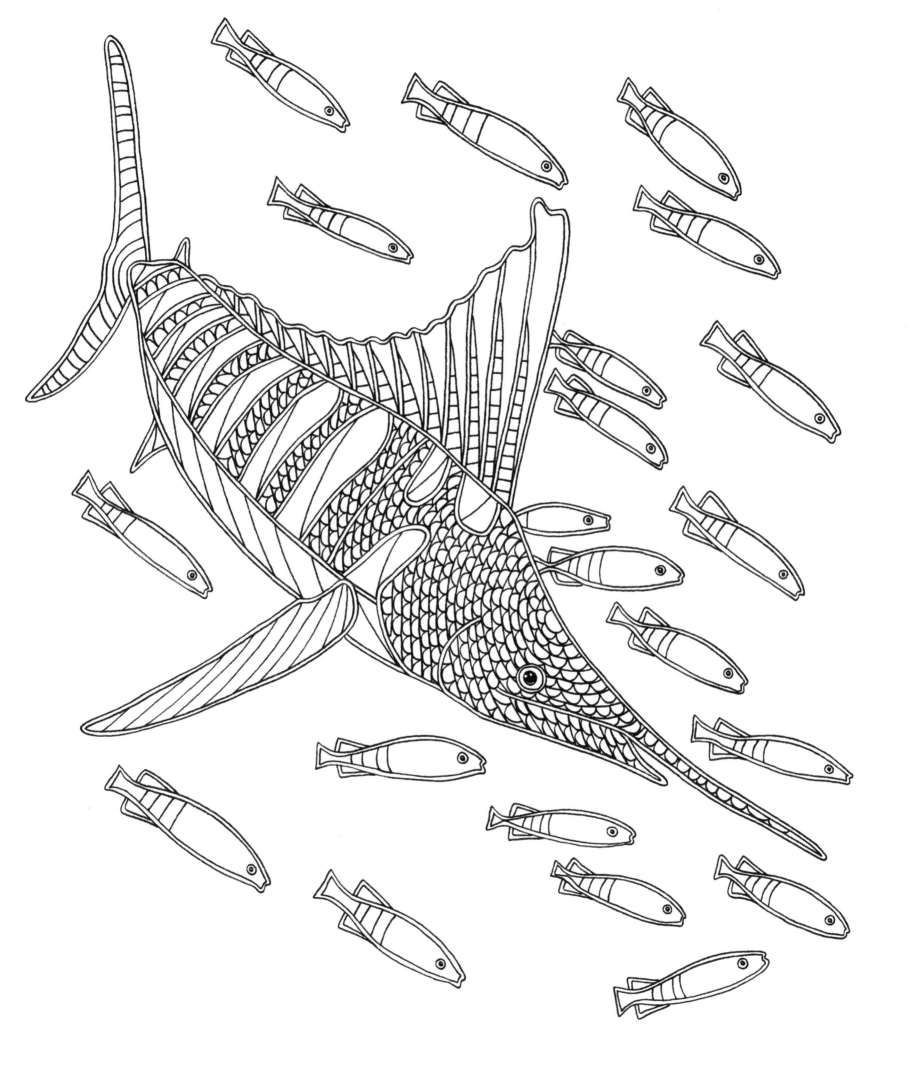

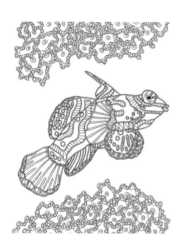

MANDARINFISH
('mand(ə)rɪnfɪʃ,' *Synchiropus splendidus*)

Truly one of the most beautiful fish in the ocean, the mandarinfish has a striking and intricate pattern. The fish are mainly bright blue and orange, but also green, purple, and yellow—they are often described as psychedelic. The mandarinfish is typically shy, and is very small in size, about 2½ in (6 cm), which can make it even harder to spot. It has a wide, square-shaped head and two leglike fins that are longer than the rest, which gives the impression that it can "walk" when swimming close to the seabed.

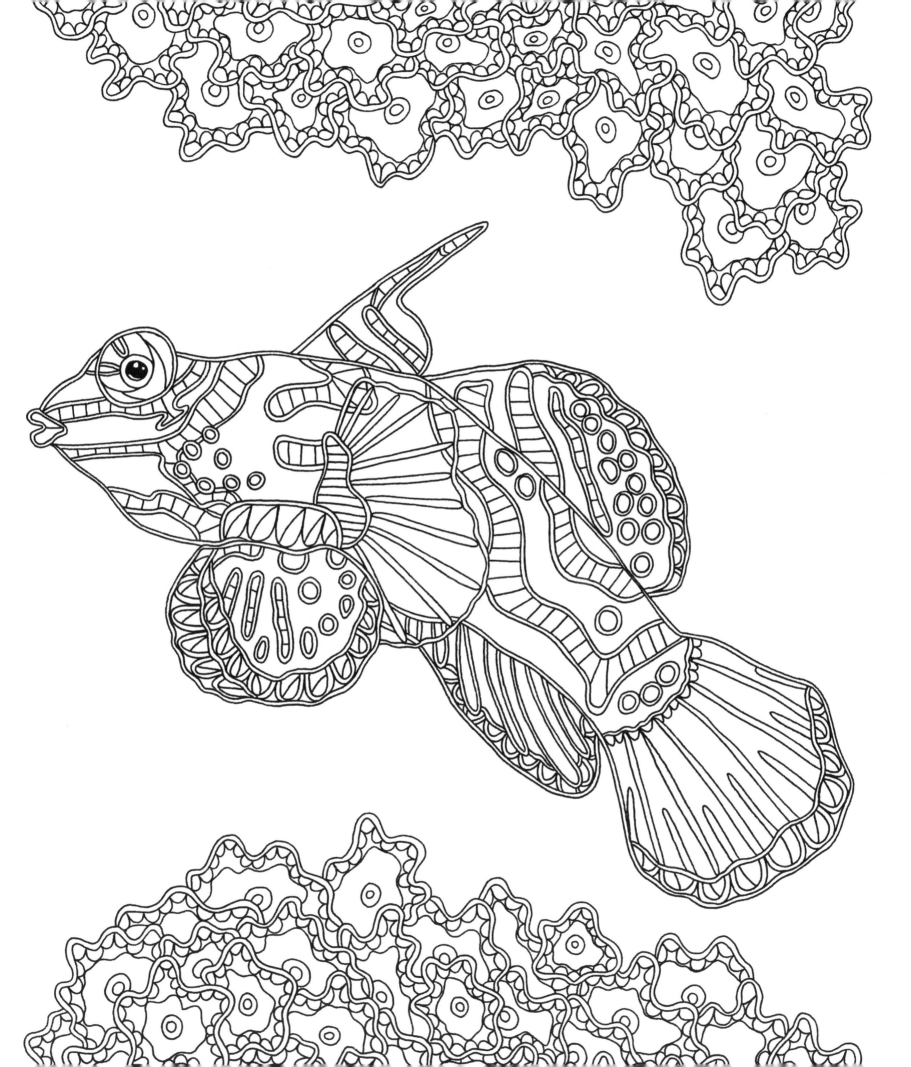

NUDIBRANCH
('njuːdɪbraŋk,' *Nudibranchia*)

These marine mollusks, or sea slugs, can survive in both cold and warm waters from the tropics to the Antarctic Ocean. Typically the size of a finger, their soft bodies crawl slowly along the ocean floor or across coral. Their main defense is to ingest toxins in the food they eat, storing and then discharging them as poison when attacked. Some species are noted for their strangely formed bodies with lumpy gills and extraordinarily contrasting color patterns, intended as a visual warning to predators signaling their toxic flesh.

Atlantic Mackerel 58

Banggai Cardinalfish 22

Bigfin Reef Squid 52

Blue Discus Fish 30

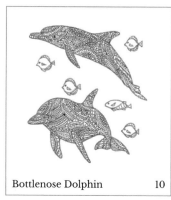

Bottlenose Dolphin 10

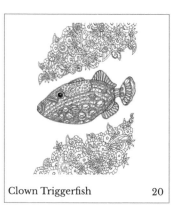

Clown Triggerfish 20

Coconut Octopus 12

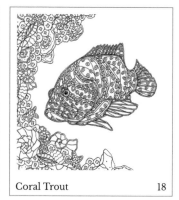

Coral Trout 18

Crown of Thorns 24

Dragon Wrasse 38

Dugong 34

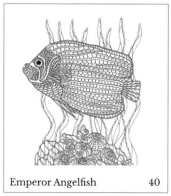

Emperor Angelfish 40

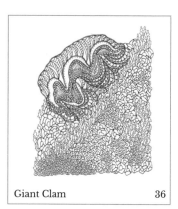

Giant Clam 36

Giant Grouper 42

Green Sea Turtle 6

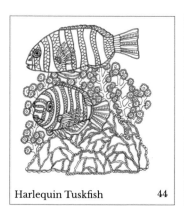

Harlequin Tuskfish 44

Hermit Crab 46

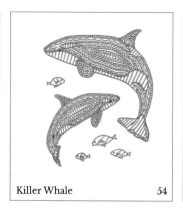

Killer Whale 54

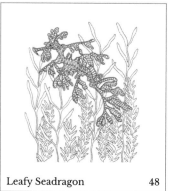

Leafy Seadragon 48

Lionfish 8

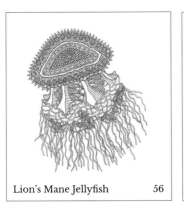

Lion's Mane Jellyfish 56

Mandarinfish 74

Nudibranch 76

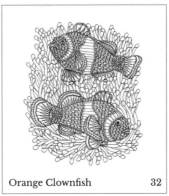

Orange Clownfish 32

Oriental Sweetlips 16

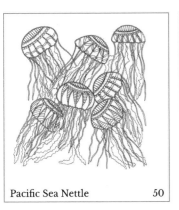

Pacific Sea Nettle 50

Peacock Mantis Shrimp 14

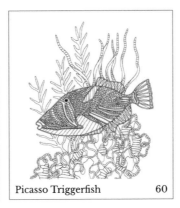

Picasso Triggerfish 60

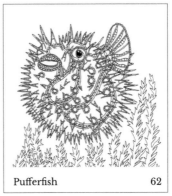

Pufferfish 62

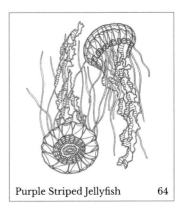

Purple Striped Jellyfish 64

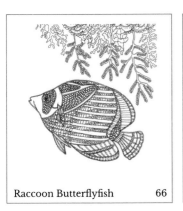

Raccoon Butterflyfish 66

Rainbow Parrotfish 68

Ribbon Eel 70

Seahorse 4

Spotted Eagle Ray 26

Spotted Trunkfish 28

Striped Marlin 72

Author's Acknowledgments
I would like to express a warm thank you to all
who have made this book possible and for the brilliant
encouragement throughout.

WATERLIFE.

For information, address St. Martin's Press, 175 Fifth Avenue,
New York, N.Y. 10010.
www.stmartins.com

Conceived and produced by
Elwin Street Limited
3 Percy Street
London W1T 1DE
www.elwinstreet.com

Library of Congress Cataloging-in-Publication Data Available
Upon Request

ISBN 978-1-250-09503-9

First U.S. Edition: March 2016

Our books may be purchased in bulk for promotional,
educational, or business use. Please contact your local
bookseller or the Macmillan Corporate and Premium Sales
Department at (800) 221-7945, extension 5442, or by e-mail
at MacmillanSpecialMarkets@macmillan.com.

10 9 8 7 6 5 4 3 2 1

Printed in Singapore